A TREE IS A PLANT

LET'S
READ
AND
FIND
OUT

A TREE
IS A PLANT

by Clyde Robert Bulla

illustrated by Lois Lignell

THOMAS Y. CROWELL COMPANY · NEW YORK

LET'S-READ-AND-FIND-OUT SCIENCE BOOKS

Editors: *DR. ROMA GANS*, Professor Emeritus of Childhood Education, Teachers College, Columbia University

DR. FRANKLYN M. BRANLEY, Chairman and Astronomer of The American Museum–Hayden Planetarium

*AVAILABLE IN SPANISH

REC Library Edition reprinted with the permission of Thomas Y. Crowell Company

Responsive Environments Corp., Englewood Cliffs, N. J. 07632

ISBN 0-690-83529-9
ISBN 0-690-83530-2 (LB)

25291

A tree is a plant.
A tree is the biggest
plant that grows.

1

oak

spruce

birch

Most kinds of trees grow from seeds
the way most small plants do.
There are many kinds of trees.
Here are a few of them.
How many do you know?

palm.

willow

This tree grows in the country. It might grow in your yard, too.

Do you know what kind it is?

This is an apple tree.

The apple tree came
from a seed.
The seed was small.
It grew inside an apple.
Have you ever seen
an apple seed?

Cut an apple in two.
The seeds are in the center.

They look like this.

7

Most apple trees come from seeds that are planted.
Sometimes an apple tree grows from a seed that falls
to the ground.

The wind blows leaves over the seed.
The wind blows soil over the seed.

All winter the seed lies under the leaves or the soil.
All winter the seed lies under the ice and snow and is pushed into the ground.

Spring comes.
Rain falls.

The sun comes out and warms the earth.
The seed begins to grow.

At first the young plant
does not look like a tree.
The tree is very small.
It is only a stem with two
leaves.

It has no apples on it.
A tree must grow up
before it has apples on it.

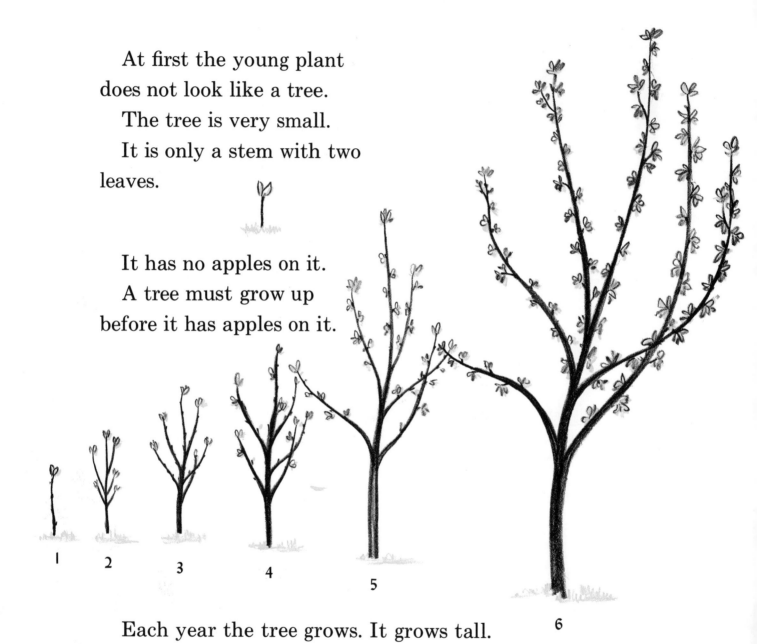

1

2

3

4

5

6

Each year the tree grows. It grows tall.

In seven years it is so
tall that you can stand
under its branches.

In the spring there
are blossoms on the
tree. Spring is
apple-blossom time.

The blossoms last only a few days.
Then they fall to the ground.

12

Now there are green leaves on the tree. Among the leaves there are small apples. The apples are where the blossoms were before. The apples are green, and they are almost too small for you to see.

The apples grow slowly.

They grow all during the spring

and all during the summer.

In the fall they are large and ripe. They are ready to eat.

We can see the apples and the leaves on the branches. We can see the branches growing out of the trunk. We can see the trunk growing out of the ground.

We can see the bark of the tree.

The bark covers the branches and the trunk like a coat.

But there is a part of the tree that we cannot see.

We cannot see the roots.

They are under the ground.

Some of the roots are large.

Some of them are small as hairs.

The roots grow like branches under the ground.

A tree could not live without roots.

Roots hold the trunk in the ground.

Roots keep the tree from falling when the wind blows.

17

Roots keep the rain from washing the tree out of the ground.

Roots do something more. They take water from the ground. They carry the water into the trunk of the tree.

The trunk carries water to the branches.

The branches carry water to the leaves.

Hundreds and hundreds of leaves grow on the branches. The leaves make food for the tree. The leaves make food from water and air. They make food when the sun shines.

The food goes into the branches. It goes into the trunk and roots. It goes to every part of the tree.

Fall comes and winter is near.
The work of the leaves is over.
The leaves turn yellow and brown.
The leaves die
                    and
                        fall
                            to the
                                ground.

21

Now the tree is bare.
All winter it looks
dead.

But the tree is not dead.
Under its coat of bark,
the tree is alive.

Spring comes again. Rain falls.

The sun warms the earth.
The tree blossoms, and new leaves grow.
As long as it lives, the apple tree grows.
As long as it lives, the apple tree blossoms
in the spring and apples grow on it.

When do you like apple trees the best:

In spring when they are covered with blossoms?

In summer when they are covered with leaves?

In winter when they are bare?

33

Or in fall when they are covered with apples?

ABOUT THE AUTHOR

CLYDE ROBERT BULLA grew up on a farm near King City, Missouri. He received his early education in a one-room schoolhouse where he began writing stories and songs. He finished his first book shortly after his graduation from high school and then went to work on a newspaper as a columnist and a typesetter.

He continued to write, and his books for children became so successful that he was able to satisfy his desire to travel through the United States, Mexico, and Hawaii. His home is in Los Angeles, and it is there that he composes his songs and writes his stories.